THE ELEVEN COMHANDMENTS?

FROM A NAKED UNSHACKLED MIND

ANNO NOMIUS

Printed in the United States of America
First Printing: 2016
ISBN 978-0-9907412-1-3

NCIPB Inc,

PO Box 123
Stevenson, CT 06491-0123

stories.ncipb.com

Preface

How many commandments were there originally? Were there really 10? Were there more or were there less? Find out what happened back then, long long ago.

The exodus and the commandments are probably the most interesting and important event of ancient times. Do the commandments have any relevance today? They probably do for some of us. Scholars, playwrights, moviemakers, actors, songwriters, singers and others have written, enacted, and shown on the silver screen both these event many, many times. It could only mean that they thought their interpretation was the right interpretation having seen all the interpretations done before them or they were just inspired. Here is celebrating all those interpretations, and to add to the confusion, one more.

A note of caution. If you are a religious nut or a Jihadist stay away from this book. If you have an open mind, are ready for the ride and have a little sense of humor read on.

This book is dedicated to the hard working citizens of the free world with an open mind and a little sense of humor. Happy Reading!

Thank you **RBD** for the checks & balances and the idea behind the illustrations.

Characters

Aaron – A smart and good-looking man and Brother of Moses. He is quick thinking, has the gift of the gab, and would articulate what Moses could not articulate. He also possessed a rod, a wooden stick that could work miracles. Alternately, he used it to herd sheep.

Miriam – Sister of Moses. A strong independent and fiery woman. The jury is still out on whom she is married to. Is it Hur or Caleb? She used the timbrel or tambourine when dancing.

Hur – Friend of Aaron and Moses. The jury is still out on whether he is the Husband or son of Miriam. A hard working, strong man always in his work overalls. He has a thing for Miriam.

Moses – A chubby, plump bald nice guy. God or someone important handed him the commandments. These commandments are followed by some of the leading religions of the world in some shape, form, or other. He too possessed a rod, a wooden stick just like Aaron. Nobody living has seen him perform any miracles with the shaft so far though.

Arron – All star American Football quarterback looking for answers on life's important questions.

Luciella – On again, off again Mayan girlfriend of Arron. An intelligent, compassionate, curious woman exploring her sexuality. She is passionate in her beliefs. She wears large glasses and has a very loud voice.

Arun – Short name of an Indo-American friend of Arron. Nerd. A logophile, he is the youngest Winner of both the national spelling bee contest and jeopardy.

Chen - Short name of a Chinese American, Buddhist friend of Arron. Nerd. Multiple times Winner of Jeopardy.

Chapter 0

The Pharaoh of Egypt, Thutmose II or it could be Amenhotep II or Ramses II was getting increasingly tired of the Jews. Unlike the rest of the subjects in the kingdom, they were a smart lot and were always demanding more as smart people usually do. The ones who were farmers would want a better price for their crop; the ones who were involved in tannery were charging an arm and a leg for tanning of skins and hides and so on. The smartest ones moved into the money lending business as they continue to even today.

The Pharaoh could not kick them out of the country as then he would be branded anti-Semitic and his assets could be frozen by the FOII (friends of Israel International) or some coalition aligned against anti-Semitism. He disliked the fact that his hands were tied and that these people were getting large in number and powerful. He had to do something. Historically, people like him had to do something when people other than him, became more powerful and successful.

To top it, the Jews were humble, peace loving people however, in more recent times there was the case of the killing of Yitzhak Rabin, the Israeli Premier, by a Jewish radical using the *din rodef*, law of the pursuer, as the excuse. There were other shooting, skirmishes with Palestinians resulting in dead people; however, the *din rodef* law really applied there since the Palestinians always attacked first, every single time and the Jews were only defending. At least that is what the Jews have claimed.

Though the perpetrator of Rabin's assassination is in jail, it is amazing how he had the power to bowl over a married woman with four kids to leave her husband to marry him. Some women simply find bad boys hot, attractive, and very bad ones enthralling and mesmerizing. Anyways that was an aberration rather than a norm of an incident in the Jewish community and we are digressing from the main story.

The Pharaoh finally got his chance to banish the Jews when plague after plague hit the country, especially in the villages where the Jewish people lived. From these villages the plague spread to the rest of the country like an epidemic. Something had to be done.

The plagues as is the nature of the beast were bad. In one of the plagues, part of the lakes and ponds, became too polluted for even the fish and frogs to survive. In a short time, the neighboring villages were flooded, with fish & frogs of all shapes and sizes, leaving the lakes and ponds in hordes, for less polluted destinations. After that came the plague of the locusts that affected crop yields as the pesky short horned grasshoppers ate everything up in their path. Practically nothing grew that year and there was a partial famine in Egypt.

Then the lice plague broke out. Part of the reason for the plague was resistance to over the counter products like RID, Clear and other pyrethrins, the other part was a particularly warm and humid post summer, a perfect environment in which lice thrive. The lice epidemic was particularly bad because it reached the royal palace.

Queen Hatshepsut or it could be Queen Nefertiti had to shave her head to get rid of the lice, twice. Hell hath no fury like a Woman forced to shave her head and twice – you are inviting mayhem.

The Pharaoh summoned all the Jews in the kingdom to gather at the main village square, in Memphis, Egypt (some say it could have been Tahrir Square, Egypt). "You" he addressed Aaron and Miriam, "this is what you wanted right? You wanted your people to be free. We have been negotiating this for quite some time now. Well, you and your people are free now." He then turned and yelled at the congregation "Get the hell outta here and take your cattle and your belongings and get out of my sight before I change my mind. We do not want your sickness and disease here. Get out." He then turned to Moses and said "*et tu*, Moses. Get out. We don't want murderers here either."

So, the Jewish people left Egypt and the land of the Pharaoh. They followed their leaders Moses, Miriam, and Aaron into the wilderness. The exodus was tough. It was uncharted territory and food and water was scarce. There were many people and resources were limited and had to be rationed.

About 2 days after the Jews left Egypt, the Pharaoh could not find his ruby sandals with diamond straps. They were a much-cherished gift he had received from his mother on his last birthday. His mother had told him that the jewels in the sandals were mined in Tanzania and then hand crafted in Egypt and that she had to spend quite a bit of time to get this custom made for him. She also told him that they had magical powers. As long as he wore them, nobody could harm him or harm Egypt.

The Pharaoh jumped to conclusion as typical war mongers do and called on his army to follow the Jews. He was sure that Moses had stolen the ruby sandals. This was not entirely without reason. In the past, Moses thought of the Pharaoh as his brother and did not think twice about taking his things without asking. Initially it started with play-things like marbles and kites and later it had extended to his royal clothes, expensive rings he wore on his fingers.

Nature in the meantime was not being kind to the Jews. The sun was beating down hard on the people and then all of a sudden, a couple of days into the exodus, there was a period of complete darkness as they encountered a solar eclipse. Not many had seen one in their lifetime and panicked. Even brave men and women panic when confronted with an unknown and unfamiliar situation.

This was followed by another rare event. Soot and dust from a giant volcano that had erupted in Santorini, Greece made its way across the Mediterranean Sea to Egypt and neighboring areas and covered the skies, obliterating the sun. There were a few days of complete darkness. Nobody could see the sun for several days and there was total chaos. Even the plants and flowers were confused.

The giant volcano also sent down tsunami like tidal waves to the area and the Reed Sea or red sea parted for about thirty minutes or so allowing for a walk on the floor of the sea. Moses saw his opportunity and led his people through this path to firmer grounds on the other side. Everyone high fived and chest bumped after they crossed the sea. It was quite an achievement.

This kind of receding seawater phenomenon is quite common in nature. Something similar happens at Hopewell rocks at the Bay of Fundy, Canada at least twice a day.

The charging army of the Pharaoh did not fare as well as Moses and his people. By the time they reached the reed sea or red sea and started crossing the floor of the sea, the tidal wave started retreating and the water swept away many of the Pharaoh's cavalry. The army retreated quickly and raised their fists at the Jews on the other side of the sea. The Jews on the other side laughed loudly and showed them the middle finger.

Needless to mention that after the Pharaoh returned to his palace he found the royal ruby sandals with diamond straps by his bedside. Maria, the housekeeper had misplaced them. He called for her beheading.

Maria and the rest of the staff tried to plead with the Pharaoh to spare her life. She was the sole breadwinner with a family of five children and a paraplegic husband who could not work. The Pharaoh did not relent.

In his kingdom, the principle of *Maat* for delivering justice was well established. Crime and associated punishments was clear. Depending on the crime the punishment could be 100 strokes of cane, branding, exile, drowning, mutilation, decapitation, being burnt alive, sold as a slave and prison time. There was punishment where nose, feet, hand was cut. The police used trained monkey and dogs to maintain law and order. Things have not changed a whole lot since, around that part of the world.

After crossing the sea, Moses and his people travelled many miles and kilometers over several days and finally set camp at the foothills of Mount Sinai.

Some say that it was not Mount Sinai but the mountain of Gebel Khashm et-Tarif or Mount

Horeb where they camped. When you go into the past there is so much trouble getting the real facts. It is the same in present times. There are many vested interests that truth seekers have to overcome to get to the brutal honest facts.

The tough times was beginning to take a toll on the Jews. People snapped and barked at each other at the slightest pretext or provocation, especially at their leaders. The berating of the leaders however, especially of Moses, was getting out of hand. The people started insulting him personally, calling him a fat slob and other derogatory names.

A man can take only so much. Initially piqued Moses was galvanized to take action. Moses told them to wait; a classic deflection strategy used by leaders around the world. He told his people he was going to go up Mount Sinai, talk to God, and come back with the next steps. The people cheered.

Coordinates - 28°32'23"N 33°58'24"E

The year was 1500 BC, well who cares. When you go that far back, it really does not matter. Then, there are some people, who care. Archaeologists, scientists, crazy anal-retentive people, who have to get the exact date and exact facts. So some of them argue the year was 1300 BC and the discussions rage on. Get some carbon dating will you and settle this one and for all.

Anyways back to the story. Moses had just lost his temper and had broken the two tablets that God or someone important had given him and he was seeking guidance on what to do next. He had come down from the mountain, and was flanked, by his brother Aaron, Sister Miriam on one side and friend Hur on the other. A jejune Moses starts talking to Aaron trying to sound upbeat.

"Yo Aaron!"

"What's up Mo?"

"1 week that's all we have. 1 week to get the commandments ready."

"Are you kidding? Why did you break them in the first place? Are you now suggesting we have to make them up?"

"Yes and I know. I am sorry I got angry and you know I have had anger issues all my life."

"Yes I know and also speech issues." Aaron let out a sigh, referring to Moses's stammering bouts when agitated. Aaron loved his younger brother unconditionally and however bad a situation, would always try to help and defend him.

"You are a dimwit." Miriam was enraged "why do you always mess up. You are responsible for this shit that all of us have had to go through. First you killed an Egyptian and got us kicked out of Egypt and now this."

Miriam was referring to the fact how she and Aaron were able to negotiate a release of all the Jews from Egypt, escaping the wrath of the Pharaoh even after Moses killed an Egyptian. She did not know that secretly the Pharaoh had wanted to get rid of the Jews anyways.

This was the kind of bashing Moses was bad at handling and would lead him to start stuttering and stammering, and put him in a state of anomia, where he could not recall the right word to use. He would then make feeble attempts of referencing, which was pathetic. Unfortunately, he did not have an Iphone and could not summon Siri to his aid for help getting the right word or phrase.

"I wa..was..Hec..H.." Moses tried to indicate the reason why he did what he did and really, he had no choice but unfortunately, nobody understood him. Also, nobody here knew the facts. The Egyptian he had killed for which he was being acclaimed as a hero, in some circles and castigated in others was really an accident.

He distinctly remembered the Egyptian guard and the farmer Jew getting into an altercation at the bar where both of them were trying to hit on the belly dancer whose name was Aeda after they had a couple of rounds of *shekar* beer.

The Jew was obviously getting the upper hand as he had more money, which he was periodically inserting into the *bedlah* belly belt of the dancer, who was gyrating and undulating her hips ever more provocatively, as more and more money kept pouring in. The guard did not like to be one-upped.

17

A fight ensued and there was betting on who was going to win the fight with the odds stacked heavily against the farmer. Then a strange thing happened, the powerful guard tripped over himself and dropped his knife. A confused Moses picked it up and then a crowd pushed him and he fell, every 290 lbs of him on the guard face down, stabbing him to death.

"So do you remember them?" Hur asked.

"Th..th.." Moses stammered pointing at his heart.

"You fucked up big time didn't you" Miriam sighed, "Guess what Aaron, Mo fucks up, and we have to fix it, again. I think given the situation. We have no choice. We just have to make up the commandments"

Hur looked at Miriam silently. He admired her but he was not sure if it was more as a son admires his mother or a husband admires his wife. He certainly was confused & the historians were not helping either. Silently he cursed them for his quandary.

Miriam stood there visibly annoyed. Like Aaron, she loved Moses. He was after all her little brother and she would do anything to protect him. He was only twenty-five and she felt the need to protect him from everything and everybody including himself. She could say whatever she wanted to him but if someone else were to speak against Moses, she would be up in arms. She was extremely protective of him.

She was less protective of Aaron. At twenty-eight, Aaron was wise beyond his years, had the street smarts, and could take care of himself. He did not need a wingman or wing woman.

Coordinates 32°00'45"N 96°25'52"W

Many hundreds of miles away and many centuries later, sometime in the 21st century; 2016 or it could be 2017 or 2030 but does it really matter? An All American boy from one of the bluest of blue state Texas was having troubles of his own. A good student and a star athlete, life at 19 was throwing Arron, curveball after curveball, and he was having trouble handling it all.

Part of the reason was he was a football quarterback and baseball was not his forte but the other reason was all this was new; he had never experienced anything like this. In addition, puberty hit him very late and he had mixed feelings with everything going on with his body as well.

First, it was his sister. He had found out she was a slut and had slept with half the town men, the other half his mother had covered. At which point his dad asked for a divorce. Well that was part of the reason; the real reason was his dad found out that he was a woman trapped in a man's body.

Then there was his Mayan girlfriend. She was cheating on him, with another woman who was black. They were having sex on a hammock, but really, what bothered him was when he caught her in a threesome having sex with two other men, ex postal workers, one black, and one white on a hammock in her backyard. He caught her red handed one afternoon when he had stopped by to drop off a parcel at her house and heard very loud noises coming from the back of the house and then he witnessed what she was up to with the two men. That vision was embedded in his memory, forever he thought.

Both these men were on the right side of sixty, and had just become eligible for social security and Medicare. She tried to tell him she was broadening her horizons, learning from more experienced people but he thought she was shitting him but he was not sure. There was also something about the Mayans and their love for the hammock that he could not fathom.

He turned to God and he thought he was getting somewhere until the pastor at his church was convicted in a child sex abuse scandal with some support from the Vatican. The next pastor was gay and he was uncomfortable with the way he talked and walked. The world around him was exploding and he needed answers...fast.

He was going to go crazy he thought and who knows pick up a gun, maybe a Bushmaster XM-15 semiautomatic rifle or AR-15 assault rifle and start shooting people in a movie theatre in downtown. Maybe he thought, he should get a rocket launcher and blow up a few towns like Sandy Hook. Nobody cared in Washington anyways.

He needed rules, rules to live by, rules handed down by God or someone important he thought, before he went crazy.

He was beginning to get confused as well. The church now, there was the Protestants and Catholics to begin with, but there was more. Independents, marginals, orthodox, Anglicans.

As he dug deeper, the list within each category was mindboggling; the Mormons, Jehovah's witnesses, Christian science, Filipino Apostolic, Chinese full gospel, Chinese neocharismatic, Messianic, Pentecostal, independent Adventists & Baptists, Independent Greek orthodox, Hidden Hindu believers in Christ, Arab charismatic, Independent Methodist, Brazilian grassroots, Nestorian, Romanian, Estonian, Bulgarian, Macedonian, Moldavian, Moravian, Lutheran, evangelicals, Mennonite, Quakers, Shakers,

Christadelphian, Swedenborgian, charismatics and the list kept going. WTF!

So many of them, more than 30000, and each had their own ways and each was evolving as well, allowing gays and lesbians, same sex marriage. He needed an anchor to hold on to, something that did not change with time or circumstances. He was having trouble reconciling with the idea of 1 Christian God and more than 30000 ways to worship him. Certainly, the way things stood it seemed the religion's direction was exclusion rather than inclusion.

He had three good friends that he hung out with and he listened to them for their counsel as well.

The first was Chinese American who was Buddhist even though his parents insisted they were from Tibet not China. His name was Chen Dong Xue Fu Xin I-Ching Hu. His name had the ring of all utensils in the kitchen falling on the floor at the same time with quarters and dimes rolling inside them. Chen used a lot of gel on his hair and the hair on his head stood out like a porcupine.

He asked Chen what was his middle name and he lost him when he started talking about how his name was based on fortune telling and *bazi* and how each word in his 8-word name was a character when paired with the five elements gold, water, wood, fire, and earth. He also mentioned in selecting his name the year, month, day and hour of his birth was important. Chen then proceeded to tell him his name Chen meant morning, Dong in his name could mean a number of things but in his case meant east. Xue meant snow, Fu meant wealthy, I- Ching was a divine text and helped provide moral decision-making, and Hu was tiger. So the literal translation would be morning east snow wealthy divine text tiger.

Unscrambled, this Chinese fortune cookie could read *the divine text says you will be a tiger of a man and will be wealthier than all the morning snow in the east.* Another fortune cookie could possibly say *the divine text says that you will be wealthy and travel east in the morning snow on a tiger.*

There is a Chinese saying "Instead of giving your child gold, teach him a skill. Instead of teaching him a skill, bestow a good name upon your child." A good name was what Chen got.

The second friend of Arron was an Indo-American. He followed the Hindu faith and his name was Arun Shankarakutty Annapalla Kerala Cochin Taj Mahal. When he asked Arun, what's up with the long name, he was told it was a long story.

The third also his on again, off again girlfriend Luciella was of mixed origins (Dad was Canadian, Mom was from Columbia, not the university, but the country), the same girl he caught cheating. She had large glasses from a very young age, which she hated, and she had a very loud voice. She worshipped the Mayan Gods, as did her parents and 11 siblings.

Coordinates - 28°32'23"N 33°58'24"E

Back in time, the commandment problem was being discussed in excruciating detail, now that Moses had lost the original ones that God or someone important had given him.

"Ok so now what do we do?" asked Aaron.

"Well its obvious isn't it? We have to get dimwit here to remember them and Hur will write them down!" said Miriam.

"Okay give me a sec. Let me get my tablet out."

Hur grabbing a stone tablet even though he would have preferred something lighter, maybe something built by Microsoft or Apple.

"By the way Mo where were you gone for 40 days? You have no idea what we had to put up with in your absence. There was an uprising of sorts and not knowing where you were we had to come up with creative ideas to manage the dissent. We had to build a golden calf and do other crazy shit to appease and control a mob, which was getting very restless. "

"Sorry, I got lost on Mount Sinai, Aaron and then

the weather got very bad and then of course there is the incident of how I got the tablets"

"Just as I expected. Anyways Hur are you ready to write?" Miriam had an acrimonious tone.

"Yes, ok Mo, what do you remember?"

Mo looked blankly at all three of them.

"Thou thou" he muttered incoherently.

Miriam was enraged. It was unusual because she already had her periods even though Donald (no relation of Donald Trump) and other elders of the community have attributed her temper or her line of questioning to that.

"You shall have no other gods before me."

Everyone looked at Aaron.

"What?" they exclaimed in unison.

"Look what are we trying to do. For people to follow us we need to be unique. We need to be the chosen people of God. The God we believe needs to be the only one, the supreme one."

"I agree not Amun, RA, ISIS, Osiris, Nut or some other Egyptian God or Pharaoh" nodded Miriam in agreement, significantly calmer now.

The five Gods that Miriam was referring to had important significance in Egyptian life or so they thought. Amun was the most powerful Egyptian God, king of the Gods. RA, the important Egyptian sun God was swallowed every night by the sky goddess Nut and reborn every morning (It certainly was quite a nutty state of affairs in the land of the Pharaohs). ISIS was the protective Goddess, who cast powerful spells to help people in need unlike the ones of recent times. Osiris, a relative of ISIS, perhaps a brother or husband, was the god of the dead and the ruler of the underworld. There certainly were more gods but these were the more important ones and thankfully, there were none named Al-Qaida.

"Also we need to make sure that the message is that there is only one God and not many like what the Egyptians believe in. Even if it is the fact the message gets lost." Added Moses, finding his voice, now that he was calmer too.

"Ok done." Hur carved out the words.

You shall have no other gods before me.

"Here's another one. **You shall not take the name of the LORD, your God in vain.**"

Aaron was on a roll.

"I like that," Miriam commented, "this way nobody argues about God and reveres him and nobody abuses him and always treats him with dignity and respect."

"Right, I think this will stop people from committing blasphemy," Hur added as he carved out the words.

"How about you shall not make idols." Miriam mused.

"Good one. This one nails it," Aaron was nodding his head, "Good one sis. This kind of builds on the earlier commandment. No idol worship as practiced by the Egyptians. We have to be unique in our message. The Egyptians are too powerful and influential. We have to give an alternative religion as a repartee to the people and stop this worship of idols of sun, moon, stone and Pharaohs as God. Our God is the one. No worshipping of any physical objects and pagan deities. I like this."

"How about some work life balance as a commandment?" Aaron mused.

"Like a holy day of worship where all you do is take rest and pray?" Miriam asked.

"Yes, so a commandment which goes like this **Remember the Sabbath day, to keep it holy**."

" Great, I like it. A day of remembrance and worship of the Lord," Hur commented as he furiously wrote down the fourth commandment.

A day of remembrance, worship, and lot of good food to eat, Moses thought rubbing his belly. A day he could walk around aimlessly, smell the flowers, enjoy a walk through the forest, throw stones into the brook, hangout with his buddies and do nothing. He liked it.

"Yes now people will be happy to know we care to not work them like slaves all 7 days but limit it to 6 days. By the way when do we stop? How many commandments should there be? Mo, do you remember how many were there in the original?"

" Four, five I really can't remember Sis."

Miriam was disgusted. "Let's make it 10. The first four are really God centric. We need some rules for society so things are under control."

"How about **Honor your father and your mother.**" Aaron mused.

"Like it. Put it down. This is good. Treat your elders with respect & regard, this way at the family level there will be moral authority and controls. Children will not revolt against their parents and other elders and listen to what they say and do what they ask. They will be good children and take care of their parents in their old age. They will be civilized human beings."

"**You shall not murder.**" Mo blurted.

"Not bad," Hur said. "Miriam should I write it down?"

"Ok," Miriam said reluctantly. Though she was irritated with Mo however, this commandment was good. This would bring some semblance of decency and order in the tribe. People will not kill each other for money or anything else.

"You shall not commit adultery." Aaron mused.

Miriam thought about that one. At thirty-two, she was not a virgin and had her fair share of lovers. One had broken both her hymen and her heart but she could not remember his name or the order the events happened not that it mattered.

She was an independent, practical woman and was not sure about this one. Would she not want to commit adultery once married? What if the man she married was boring or had ED or she had a booty call and the husband wasn't there, fighting some stupid war in Afghanistan, Iraq, Iran, or Syria? What if she wanted to have a fling to spice things up (the popular magazine Cosmo says to do so but then she was getting too far ahead of her times).

"I don't know," she muttered under her breath.

"I think this is a good rule," Mo said. "This will stop people sleeping with someone else's partner and will bring order amidst chaos. This will create an honest pure society, built on solid values and respect. This will prevent possible creation of illegitimate children. There will be order. The benefits are huge. Should we go a step farther and ban kissing and making out also."

"No, I think this is it. Let's not go overboard"

"Ok, I am writing this down."

"How about **you shall not steal**," mused Aaron.

"Excellent" said everyone in unison.

Hur hurriedly wrote down the eighth commandment.

"Taking this up a few notches, how about **you shall not covet.**"

"Like it" Miriam exclaimed. "This will stop people in their tracks before they even think about stealing. This is huge no shoplifting, no looting - stop the thoughts before thoughts become action"

Aaron was stroking his chin, "Exactly."

"All right. Are we done?"

"One more to go," Hur was furiously hammering the chisel.

Mo was speaking thoughtfully "**You shall not bear false witness against your neighbor.**"

"Nice one bro," Aaron gave Mo a fist bump.

Miriam mused. It was a good one even though it came from Mo. It would bring order in society. Neighbors will not falsify claims against each other and treat their neighbors as they treat someone their own. The pressures on the courts of law will be less.

"Sure put it down," she said.

"Ok," Hur started hammering away. "It will take me couple of days to complete this now that I have the outline drafted. I think I will put five of the commandments on one tablet and the other five on the other."

"Sounds good," everyone said in unison.

Mo and Aaron retreated to their tents. En route Mo took out his shaft, Aaron took out his rod, and they playfully sparred with each other.

"Tell me about what happened on the mountain and how you got the tablets"

"I will"

Miriam hung around watching Hur. He was tall, dark handsome and had broad shoulders and very strong arms. Hur took out the first of the larger tablet where the final version was going to go, and started working on it. The sound of hammer and chisel filled the air.

Miriam felt a shiver run through her spine as she saw the sweat glistening on Hur as he worked. She felt a familiar stirring, a warmth, and moistness between her legs. She wanted to hold him and feel him against her.

Miriam started swaying to the sound of hammer and chisels and very soon found a rhythm in the sound and started dancing in circles. At times, she picked up the timbrel or tambourine in her hand to add flavor to her dancing. She was lost in her dance.

For seven days, as Hur worked, Miriam danced. The times she stopped to take a break, Miriam would make mad, passionate, mind-blowing love to Hur.

What bothered Hur was every time, right before she would have an orgasm, she would shriek "Caleb." He was not sure what to make of it but those old confusing feelings of what he meant to her returned. He cursed the historians under his breath.

Coordinates 32°00'45"N 96°25'52"W

Back to the present times, a disturbed Arron was seeking answers. He met many a religious leader and curiously enough, they had very little solid advice. They always asked for 10 % of the money he made as a quarterback, at the university in College Station, Texas, he was going to, to get a degree in sports management. They said they needed this payment to provide him with their expert advice.

He turned to the non-Christian faiths. He spoke with an Imam at a mosque and a few Rabbis and in one-way or form, they all alluded to the commandments as the rules one should live by, but they were the conduit of deliverance, the gatekeeper if you will to God's kingdom. He did not like that.

He tried to get in touch with the new Pope after all the sex scandals but learnt he was on tour. He came back skeptical about the whole papacy.

Just like in corporate America, the answer to a scandal was change in leadership. The papacy was no different. He however had some hope for both the church and the new pope because he was saying all the right things and doing all the right things. The pope even drove a small car on his last visit to the USA and last quarter profits of the Vatican were significantly up, because now they were efforts to report them accurately unlike earlier when there were efforts to underreport them. The Vatican took the teaching of *do not let your left hand know what your right hand is doing* literally.

Chen arranged for a Skype call with the Dalai Lama but Arron was not impressed. The man seemed nice but did not have the answers he was seeking. In addition, he had a hard time believing someone who could not deliver his own people. He wondered about the Lama's strategy of non-violence. Does successful non-violence movement only work in warm countries like South Africa, India, or perhaps it needs a critical mass, he wondered or a sympathetic media?

Arun organized a meeting with the son of Swami Rama, an Indian God man. He was a nice person but he was more interested in bashing his Dad than any discussion on life's pressing questions or how his Dad was able to control his heartbeat, blood pressure and other involuntary bodily process and he did not blame him. In his place, he would have done the same. Swami Rama was known to have an overactive libido and partake in lecherous behavior. He was no different from Osho Rajneesh, another Indian God man.

Luciella tried to tell him about the Mayan culture and gods in case they could provide him answers. With an intellect as sharp as his, he found the belief of worshipping dead ancestors for deliverance hard to swallow and how was the shaman any different from the priests, imams, rabbi asking for stuff, to get you in touch with God? In addition, he found the 13 levels of heaven and 9 levels in the underworld hogwash and the human sacrifices appalling. The only thing cool he thought was Acan, the God of alcoholic beverages and Acat, the tattoo God.

Frustrated he looked at his options. None of them was yielding him any answers. He thought maybe he should make a list of his questions and what was really bothering him, some of which he had posted to the people with religious authority he had met without any satisfactory answers.

What are the rules than one should live by?
Why someone is created a man, but really is a woman?
Why are there so many religions?
Is there a God and has anyone seen it?
Why do people cheat on their partners?
Why does one have a desire to have sex?
Is it ok for men to marry men and women to marry women?
Are there Karmic effects and what are the time frames?

He called on his friends to see if they had any answers.

"Well, some of the right things to do are in the commandments" Chen said. "At least what not to do, the why is not covered very well though and is up to interpretation."

"I don't know Chen. Look at the commandments. It looks so irrelevant in the modern context. Take the first one. **You shall have no other gods before me**. What does this mean? We know that there are so many religions following their own God so who is this God, before whom there are none?"

"Yes, it is very vague and unfortunately I don't have much on this. As I was saying earlier the why is not covered. People just blindly repeat the commandments as parrots, even the so-called scholars. I looked and I did not find anyone doing any in depth study. Even it seems there is not one God. Judaism for instance has seven names for god Tetragrammaton, El, Elohim, Eloah, Elohai, El Shaddai, and Tzevaot and then there is an eighth one Jah."

"Elohai sounds so much like what the Muslims call God. Allah. Interesting"

"Also if you are talking about monotheism, the concept of one God; there was an Egyptian Pharaoh who believed in the concept of one God, Akhenaten. So why breakaway from the Egyptians if they believed in one God? Akhenaten, by the way is the father of Tutankhamen and husband of Nefertiti, both famous in their own right."

"Interesting that a significant number of the Hebrew God names start with an E." Luciella observed.

"E-ya"

"By the way how many religions are there in the world currently following their own idea of a God?"

"A lot of religions exist. There are obviously the major ones with more followers. Christianity, Islam, and Hinduism are followed by about a third, a fifth, a seventh of the world population respectively. Then from all around the world you have Baha'i, Buddhism, Confucianism, Judaism, Jainism, Shinto, Sikhism, Taoism, Wicca, Zoroastrianism, and Druidism. Obviously, this is not the end all, there are more."

"Wow. I do recognize some of them. I know Baha'i. It is probably the most modern of the religions, and it originated in the Middle East Iran."

"I think it is an interesting all encompassing religion teaching world peace, democracy, civil rights, equal rights for women, the acceptance of scientific discoveries, definitely decades ahead of its time. The fact it believes in all the other religions leaders before it and their teachings is amazing. Iran has been very broadminded until now I guess."

"Yes, Zoroastrianism originated there as well. If you look at ancient history, around the times of the mighty Greeks, Persians have been very inclusive. Even though they practiced their own religion back then they allowed others to practice their own religion in their kingdom and did not persecute them for that. People spoke multiple languages and Persia was a seat of great learning. As a matter of fact in excavations in Persepolis, Iran there are artifacts depicting people of other nations coming to the kingdom of Persia bearing gifts and these people were not depicted in chains, as slaves, as in some of the other nations of the time but rather as equals."

"Hey even some of the Greeks wanted the Persians to rule them. They were getting fed up with their rulers and their rules"

"Wow such great leaders and such great thoughts. I wish I was living then and listening to these great men and women talk. Cyrus the great from Persia in ancient times delivered the Jews from Babylonian captivity I have read."

"Yes unlike now where they are constantly at each other's throats, back then Israel and Iran were in very good terms and very respectful of each other."

"Ok let's look at the next commandment. The next one is as bad. **You shall not make idols.** Well there are idols all around of Christ, Mary, the manger and others so what is the idea? If not idols, there are symbols. There is the hexagram of the Star of David; cross of Christ and the list is long. So this whole idea of not making idols is a misnomer."

"The next one makes no sense either. **You shall not take the name of the LORD your God in vain**. People swear on God's name and take his name in vain all the time. When they are driving and someone cuts in front of them, when they accidently cut themselves with a knife, on roller coaster rides, making out or making love."

"I could rattle off numerous other examples. What is the point of the commandments, which are not implementable and there are no repercussions if you break them?"

"Yes, I think you may have a point there. Perhaps they are just directives. I know of a lot of people who do not follow the commandments and seem to be doing all right, very well in some cases, at least from the outside, in my perspective."

"Does anyone know what this means? **Remember the Sabbath day, to keep it holy**."

"Oh," Luciella exclaimed, "That's a day of religious observance and abstinence from work. Jews do that starting Friday into Saturday and Christians on Sunday. I am guessing the Muslims do this on Friday"

"That is right but then Pottery Barn, Pier One, Macy's, Target are open all seven days so how is this implementable? Or maybe there is exclusion for businesses?"

"Interesting, is that why at least most work place have holidays on Saturday and Sundays? I thought it had something to do with labor laws and 40 hour work week, but even then those two days of rest could have been Monday and Tuesday."

"Yes, it is a religious thing"

"Now, how about this? **Honor your father and your mother.** These days we leave them to die at the old age homes, nursing homes where some stranger takes care of them. I understand we have work and other stuff we have to do which prevents us from taking care of them fulltime and just visit them on weekends. So do we just need to Honor and respect them as long as they are useful/fit?"

"That's not true where there is strong family values and culture. Not in my culture" quipped Luciella "We take care of family within the family as much as possible. In addition, healthcare is expensive, so it is cheaper to take care of a person at home. We respect and honor our elders and ancestors"

"Well that's because you have a large family and lot of help and also your family is not as screwed up as mine."

"So? It's the intent that matters. Typically when someone falls sick all the friends drop off once the going gets tough and finally it's really family and one or two close friends who stick. You realize then that 99% of your so-called friends are fair weather friends. Anyways it's a matter of perspective. I think that for me I would like to take care and honor my parents in good times and bad. I want them with me not away from me so I can have a good time. Unlike you, I am not from the me culture. I care deeply about others," Luciella barked loudly at Aaron.

"whoa, whoa back off. This is a discussion. Let's be civil"

Aaron was shaken. Luciella was a spitfire when she got into a discussion she cared passionately about and would rip people apart on the other side of the discussion and then she had a loud voice, double whammy.

"All right, this one I get. **You shall not murder**. You should not kill another person for any reason. However, this one is questionable in current times. **You shall not commit adultery**."

Arron gave Luciella a hard look and she winced. Payback time.

"I get this, this one is obvious. **You shall not steal**."

Arun nodded in agreement. Chen nodded because he was not sure and Luciella kept quiet.

As a young girl when she did not know better, she had shoplifted a couple of times. Over time, it had become such a bad habit that sometimes she would do it without the need to, just for the thrill of the challenge. She and the people she associated with at that time enjoyed the thrill of breaking rules.

"Now what does this do? **You shall not bear false witness against your neighbor**. Just say, do not lie, why this elaborate make up. It almost sounds like a lawyer made it up."

"Let's look at the last one. **You shall not covet.** That is not implementable and not right. We have TV, radio the Internet, and all the advertisement usually in our face and there is no way we can watch that and not covet anything. We see something and we want it. I see a picture of a nice car, I want it. I see bread, cake and I want to eat it."

"Well there is that but there is the good covet. You see someone doing something well and getting ahead and are motivated to be like that. This needs some clarification. It seems to me that the commandments were written in a particular context which we are missing"

"Yes agreed," Chimed Arun, "also some of the questions you are asking isn't covered. I have a few questions of my own."

"What kind?" asked Luciella.

"Why did my Dad die so young?"

Luciella started brooding "Yes why are our loved ones snatched away from us. I miss my Mom"

"My brother Liam is dead"

Everyone was quiet. Chen's brother Liam had died Sept 11 2011. Arron for a second forgot his troubles, went over, and hugged Chen. Arun and Luciella followed. Nobody realized it but Chen was just stating a fact, he had alexithymia and could not comprehend some of the emotional behaviors of his friends let alone his own.

Coordinates - 28°32'23"N 33°58'24"E

Aaron and Moses were talking to each other.

"So tell me what happened. How did you get those tablets?"

"Well like I was saying earlier, I got lost in the mountain and kept wandering through them for a very long time, till I got to a clearing. You know how the mountain is barren but this place was green, there were flowers and there was a clear stream. I took off my clothes and started taking a bath. All of a sudden, the sky turned pitch dark and I could feel the droplets of rain on my skin but soon the weather turned nasty and the rain came down hard. I ran for cover under a tree and watched the thunder and lightning. It seemed it would never end."

"All of a sudden, in the water, I saw a spherical white glow with a bluish tinge. It was faint at first but then began to grow and also kept moving forward until it became very big and was less than 20 feet from where I was. It was hard to look at. The rays coming from the glow was sharp, soothing nevertheless. I felt happy for no apparent reason. I knew this was unusual. It probably was God or someone important. All of a sudden two pieces of stone tablets fell out of the glow and I heard a booming voice **take these to your people…and cover yourself up will you** and then the glow disappeared."

"Wow"

"Yes, wow indeed. Also, I am not sure if I heard the sound or was it implanted in my head. I had not eaten a good meal in quite a few days and was hungry and thirsty so could have been delusional."

"Right however you are one lucky bastard to see such a wonderful sight"

"Anyways I took the 2 stone tablets and suddenly I remembered where I was and how to get back home. I think the stone tablets had some mystical powers"

"What happened then?"

"Well" Mo was sheepish. "It was getting dark. I was carrying the stone tablets down the mountain to get home and I heard noises, as I got closer to the village. I realized it was revelry and I got irritated as I watched my people eating, drinking, and dancing with merriment. Here I was, hungry, thirsty and there they were having fun. Here I was, spending 40 days and 40 nights, looking for answers for them and there they were, dancing with no cares about the world and certainly not me."

"I did not realize you took it so hard"

"That's when I lost it and smashed the tablets, and then took out a hammer and broke them into more and more pieces till they were dust. You know how much of a party animal I am and not being invited to the party was too much. It is not the dancing I care about, you know I cannot dance, but it is the good food that I miss. The lovely sweet manna bread, the matzoh ball soup, cholent, they are so yummy." Mo was salivating just thinking about the food.

"Dude you certainly have a temper. Yes, we did have those on the menu. We also had borekas, Kugel, and the spicy shakshuka"

"Oh, so you had more food. Yes, I know about my temper, but as soon as I broke the tablets, I realized how wrong it was and now we have seven days to come up with the new ones. I hope Hur finishes carving them out soon. I need to lead my people to the Promised Land."

"Promised land?"

"Yah dude, Man's gotta live somewhere. I am just going to say to my people that God has told me about the promised land where all of us are going to live and I was told this when the commandments were given to me."

"Wouldn't that be a lie? But I guess leaders have to lie, make promises during election seasons and for other reasons all for the greater cause"

49

"Yes leaders have an obligation to the people, buy the people and perhaps for the people"

Aaron was not aware of the Gettysburg address so did not get it, so changed the subject, however back of his mind he felt what was said back then was being manipulated here.

"Well while you were gone, the people were getting angsty. They thought you would return soon with God or God's message and you were long gone. There was an uprising. I had to use my rod and turn it into a snake to scare them. When that did not work, I turned their drinking water to blood to teach them a lesson."

"Really you can do that!"

"Well not really. It was more of a trick I played. To turn the water red though I had to release pfisteria, an algae which kills fish, and turns the color of the water red from the blood of its victims."

"That kind of worked to get them to listen to me and then I built them a golden calf and told them that this is God"

"What and how?"

"Yes. Miriam and I asked the people to give us whatever gold they possessed. People obliged.

With the help of Hur, we built an intense fire to melt the gold to make it malleable and turn it into the shape of a Golden Calf. That made them happy and then we had a big party to celebrate."

"Ok the party that pissed me off? Anyways we will need to fix that. As an idol, the golden calf does not jive with the commandments. I am pretty sure if we don't destroy it now someone in the distant future may be inspired, maybe on wall street, Manhattan or somewhere, will mimic it and who knows make it look like a bull and that would not be good."

Aaron nodded "People are crazy. They may then climb on it, take pictures of it, take selfies with it and then tweet or instagram it. We should do everything we can to prevent the spread of that kind of BS."

"Yes, especially when people use your art and never pay for it. Not even the city. How does it make an artist feel?"

"Undervalued and unappreciated."

Aaron and Moses were talking about the bull in downtown Manhattan, around Wall Street. This was created and installed after the recession of 1989, by an artist; however, the city never paid him for the work. Granted the city never asked him to make it but when you are making millions from tourists coming in to see it, there should be some acknowledgement and financial compensation.

Coordinates 32°00'45"N 96°25'52"W

Arun Shankarakutty Annapalla Kerala Cochin Taj Mahal was in a pensive mood. He missed his Dad. His Dad was a good man. A doctor by profession, he was good at his job, was well respected, and liked however; he had not been good in maintaining his own health.

His uncontrollable eating habits, ice cream, and Künefe in particular, led to his diabetes and subsequent renal failure and death. The money that he had made was consumed by the dialysis machine and medication in his final years. There was not much left; except the house, that Arun and his mother lived in. He wiped a tear. He did have a few questions for God. Thankfully, he had a scholarship to MIT, where he was majoring in physics and for what was not covered, he had a job at the MIT lab.

Chen Dong Xue Fu Xin I Ching Hu was crying. All his life he had trouble dealing with his alexithymia. It had been a couple of years since his older brother's death but it was not clear if that is why he was crying. Like Arun, Chen was majoring in physics at Rice University but unlike him, he was not on a scholarship, but he paid in-state tuition. He could be crying for that. He certainly was very competitive.

Chen's mom never fully recovered from Liam's death and his Dad had his fast food Chinese restaurant that helped him cope with the loss. When your delivery motto is "ni chi guo le ma? Food be ready in 10-15 minutes," you do not have time, even to brood over the death of your first-born. His mom never understood why her older son was so obsessed with skydiving.

Chen knew he would now never know where his brother kept his issues of playboy. Chen wiped a tear.

Luciella did have one thing to ask God. Why she could not be with her Mom and siblings? Though she was born in the US of A, just like her other friends, America was a strange country.

A country, built on the hard work of the immigrants, had kicked out her Mom and siblings citing they were illegal immigrants even though her mom was living and working for more than 30 years in the country and had come in legally.

Unfortunately, she lost all her documentation and so did the immigration department when the last tornado hit Love County, Oklahoma, where she was living at that time. Her eleven siblings lost their documentation in a fire, couple of years back, so were deported as well with her mom.

She and her Canadian Dad could stay because she had the legal documents to show that she was born here. Luckily, for her the fire did not destroy her documents. Her Dad could stay because he was white even though he was an illegal immigrant. He did have to forge some documents about his legal residency to get a job in the postal department. He had Bonnie & Clyde Inc to help him with that.

Her Dad grew up in Manitoba, Canada in an Indian reservation and was adopted by an Indian family when his Caucasian mother abandoned him at birth. He came to the US illegally looking for work.

Luciella wondered why the law enforcement officers always asked for immigration documents from anyone looking or talking different from them which in Texas meant only one thing, being non-white.

They do not do this to the Canadians she thought. She also thought about Arron. She could not understand why Arron was hung up about whom she slept with. She was exploring her sexuality and wanted to see what it felt like to sleep with both men and women. Neither experience was particularly exciting to write home about especially the last three-some where she slept with two of her retired father's colleagues from the post office.

In all the cases, she could remember, where she slept with someone, it started with the connection. She would start listening intently to the tales of sorrow and woe that the person would relate, she would then put her arms around the person to comfort them, one thing would lead to another, usually fondling followed with more intense groping, and the bed or hammock would start rocking soon after. It was only with Aaron it always started with a meaningful kiss and handholding. He would then serenade to her with the familiar war cry *Hullabaloo, Kanek! Kanek!* This would always make her feel special.

She tried to tell Arron it was no big deal, she only loved him, and that was all that mattered but Arron seemed distrustful and did not love her back as he used to.

She did not tell him that she chose to get a degree in Urban and Regional Planning at the same university that Aaron went to, so she could be close to him. She wiped a tear.

Back at the corner, Aaron wiped a tear. He was beginning to realize he was not going to get the answers he was seeking.

Coordinates - 28°32'23"N 33°58'24"E

It was the seventh day since Hur put the first chisel and hammer on the tablet. As he lay on the ground, with Miriam on top, he admired his completed work. The commandments were ingrained in the two tablets. It looked nice he thought.

"Hur," Miriam said lazily, laying there naked with the kind of enervation right after sex.

"Yes dear"

"Don't you think there should be an 11th commandment honey?"

"An 11th commandment?"

"Yes **love**, the 11th commandment .Just love. Do you think you can add that for me sweetie pie"

"Sure" there was no hesitation in Hur's voice. You do not argue with someone, you are getting it from, you oblige him or her or both.

No one knew but at twenty-eight, Hur was a virgin until now. The last seven days were heaven as he learnt the art of lovemaking from a much-experienced older Woman. Until this experience, He was not even aware that there were more positions than one and this woman has taught him quite a few in seven days.

He got up as did Miriam, carved the 11th commandment on a new tablet, and stepped back to admire his work.

Miriam turned his face towards her and kissed him. "How many times will you admire the commandments? You need to pay me some attention," She said playfully.

She reached down and grabbed his manhood. Hur immediately got an erection. Miriam pushed him to the ground, adjusted herself on top of his erection, and slowly pushed herself, until she completely engulfed him and then very deliberately started rocking back and forth, slowly at first and then faster and faster.

The saga lasted exactly seven minutes. Yet again, she shrieked "Caleb, Caleb, Caleb" as wave after wave of orgasms engulfed her.

Hur could not help it but found his manhood recoiling and losing its poise at each utterance of that name. Who is Caleb? He wondered.

Was Miriam cheating on him mentally? Was she fucking him or fucking with him? He made up his mind to ask her about the Caleb guy when she was less aggressive and mellow which he knew would be difficult. However, he had to do this. This thing was driving him nuts and leaving him very confused and frustrated.

Coordinates 32°00'45"N 96°25'52"W

Arron woke up happy. A good night sleep helps solve problems in mysterious ways. The drinking and the good time at the local cabaret, Wispers, last night, certainly helped.

Crystal, in her short high school girl outfit and red high heels, knew how to show Arron a good time. She certainly helped clear his head. He now knew what he had to do.

Sometime you have to leave a problem alone and come back to it, later, with a new perspective.

He summoned his friends for breakfast over at Whataburger. They made the best pancakes and egg sandwich in town. He was dying for a good meal. Thinking made him hungry.

"Guys I have an idea to get the questions we have been asking answered."

"You do!" everyone exclaimed in unison.

"Yes, we just need to find out how the commandments were written. Find the people who wrote them and that should give us some answers and next steps. Perhaps when we meet them we can ask them the other questions that are bothering us."

"The commandments were written thousands of years ago."

"Agreed but aren't you guys doing some cutting edge research on time travel"

It was true. Chen and Arun were involved in some path breaking research on time travel, a joint collaboration between MIT and Rice University. Some of the concept experiments were being conducted at MIT but the more detailed experiments with animals as subjects was being conducted at Rice.

"But, but our research is on going forward in time to the future not the past. Also, we did run two successful experiments one on a mouse and one on a monkey. Human experiments are premature."

"Well you guys figure this out. This is our only chance. I am willing to help."

"Me too!" Luciella exclaimed.

Arun and Chen agreed reluctantly. All the hoops that would need to be crossed, to make this happen, was overwhelming to put it relatively.

They cursed Einstein and other theoretical physicists under their breaths. They just said stuff, wrote some equations, and presented some papers with a great deal of conviction. Their colleagues would then come out and support the ideas because in some cases, they did not quite understand what they were trying to say and did not want to appear like fools.

Then it was all upon the experimental physicists like them to prove those theories. This was true about Einstein as well. There were astronomers and physicists ducking bullets, prison, and wars taking pictures of solar eclipses and such in places in Europe, US and as far as Australia to prove his theories.

Coordinates - 28°32'23"N 33°58'24"E

"So are you done Hur?"

"Yes"

"Ok let's go. Follow me"

The four of them started to head towards the makeshift village. Hur had the three tablets on his back as they briskly walked towards the village square. Unbeknownst to him, one of the tablets that he was carrying fell on the ground.

A crowd was forming at the village square. Word had spread like wildfire that Moses had brought with him the words, the commandments, from the creator of the world.

The four of them arrived at the village square and congregated around the mound. Aaron climbed up the mound and began to speak.

"Moses is back!"

Everyone cheered. The crowd was now growing as Aaron continued to speak.

"Moses has returned after 40 days and 40 nights and he has words from the mouth of the Lord. He travelled high and low on the mountain seeking the lord to find answers, to help you, his people and did finally get to meet with the lord."

"I present to you the chosen one of the Lord, Moses," Aaron ended eloquently.

There was applause. Aaron descended from the mound and Moses galumphed over to the mound, started to get up, and slipped. It had rained the night before. He fell hard on his buttocks, yelled, and farted simultaneously.

"Ow! Ow!"

Everyone laughed. Hur tried to help Moses up but he brushed aside the help and tried again. This time he succeeded and began to speak.

"Friends Israelites and countrymen. I come before you to praise the lord not to bury him. I come to tell you I have seen him and he is real."

The place was packed by now. Everyone and his or her mother were there. They were listening intently to what Moses had to say but quickly realized he was rambling. He did not have the gift of the gab like his brother and was not impressive at all. Then to add to the rambling, was the stuttering and stammering midsentence, which was driving them nuts.

A few tried throwing rotten tomatoes and eggs at him but it did not reach him so he did not get the message and continued to ramble and stammer.

"And finally," he said dramatically. "I present to you the commandments from God"

There was commotion and cheering as Hur pulled out the tablets from his rucksack. He only found two. Where did the third one go? Miriam was looking at him intently. In the interest of time and the moment, Hur handed over the tablets to Moses.

Moses picked the first tablet and raised it high above his head.

"Here is the first set of commandments."

The people cheered. He read each one aloud and there was loud cheers as he read each. After reading the five inscribed commandments, he laid it upright on the ground for all to see. He then took out the second tablet and proceeded to repeat the exercise. There was pandemonium.

Amidst the entire hullabaloo, Miriam glared at Hur. Hur sheepishly looked away. He could not look Miriam in the eye, now that he had lost the third tablet, which had the 11th commandment. Under normal circumstances, he would have found those eyes pretty.

Moses raised his hand. The noise subsided.

"I have more news"

The people were listening intently.

"The Lord has promised us a land, only for us. A land, which is ours and ours alone, not owned by the Egyptians or anyone else for that matter. A land flowing with milk and honey"

He paused for effect. The people were all ears. Some in the audience were wondering if Moses had gone nuts. They had plenty of goats to give them milk. Thankfully, the Pharaoh had allowed them to take their cattle with them. Also for honey, they had many portable beehives that they were carrying with them. They were not sure why

Moses was trying to entice them with milk and honey.

"In 7 hours we will leave this place and head over yonder. Pack your bags and make sure you carry with you your clothes, all important documents and also don't forget your tooth paste, tooth-brush, & soap." Moses pointed out into the desert.

There was a huge uproar amongst the people especially from the Amelekite section of the crowd. They did not like what they were hearing. Everyone felt very comfortable here and to move all over again! They also were not buying into the milk and honey story.

Nobody likes change. This news was shocking even to Miriam and Hur, and to some extent Aaron. They dispersed into the crowd to do some damage control because the crowd was getting very unruly. Some of the Amalekites were outraged and wanted to kill Moses. They did not consider him their leader even though God had said he was their leader and had given him the 11 commandments minus one.

Aaron and Hur took the Amalekites down one by one as they brandished their sword, using just their rod and knife, while Miriam used her Karate punch and Jujutsu moves to silence Moses's critics. A few got a hard kick in the groin or had their balls squeezed until they withered and doubled up in pain crying for mercy.

Moses just stood there with his arms raised as the uprising subsided and looked at his arms with narcissistic admiration and marveled at his powers.

Here is where many a leader goes wrong. Moses thought he had miraculous powers and he could stop wars by just raising his hands but really, it was someone else, doing the behind the scenes work, to create that illusion. In this case, it was very clear it was Aaron, Hur, and the fiery Miriam.

Coordinates 29.7169° N, 95.4028° W

The four of them drove down in Luciella second hand Nissan Versa to Houston, Texas. It was a good 3-hour drive. There was not a whole lot of planning that went into the trip. They just threw their clothes, some documents, toothpaste toothbrush, and soap in the trunk of the car and went.

There, at the Rice university lab that summer the four of them were huddled over the experimental gadget that had successfully sent a mouse and monkey into the future. The mouse returned but the monkey did not however they had inferential data that proved that the monkey was indeed in the future. Why the monkey did not come back was up for debate but one of the hypotheses was that he found the future more interesting than the present.

"So how does this time travel concept work and how is this machine going to help us get there?"

"Well the idea is simple. You know speed is distance divided by time. Also time is distance divided by speed"

"Isn't that one and the same thing?"

"Yes it is but just wanted everyone to understand. Now if I as an observer was watching you and you were to walk to New Orleans versus Luciella who is on a flight to New Orleans Luciella will take less time to travel the same distance"

"Isn't that obvious. She is on an airplane"

"Yes, Yes. So Luciella is younger than you relatively and time passes slower for her."

"What, that's baloney. I prefer the explanation of space-time continuum"

"Well that's the concept on which this contraption was built"

"So would that mean that pilots and air hostesses who travel a lot more and faster than everyone else, almost every day of the year, are younger than the average folks"

"Yes"

"Wow, so it's that and not the anti aging wrinkle creams which is the secret to youth."

"Anyways, so what this gadget does is, it spins at very high speed, clockwise, close to the speed of light and drops you into the future"

"Ok so to go into the past the gadget would need to spin at a very high speed, anticlockwise?"

"Correct that would be the expectation. Also until now we were just transporting in the future, the location was unchanged. We will need to modify the machine to change the location to point to the location where the commandments were produced by Moses"

"Ok then let's give this a shot"

A few adjustments was made to the gadget for the location and to make it spin counter clock wise and a camera was fit in the device so it could take pictures and send back from the past. The gadget was set in motion. The four waited eagerly for the pictures. When the pictures came, it did not make sense. They were looking at a mountain in the Middle East and people who looked futuristic. Everyone was flummoxed.

"What happened here? Did we make a mistake?"

"Yes, let's get back to the basic and understand the relativity theory and what it means properly and apply it. I wish we had a theoretical physicist amongst our midst. We are experimentalists and can only try this and try that and hope, like car mechanics at the gas station, while the mechanics at the car manufacturer has the entire picture."

For the next several days, the four of them were huddled in the lab trying to figure out a way to go back in the past.

They read what Einstein had inferred long long ago. They seemed like three innocuous statements.

Laws of physics are the same for all non-accelerating observers

Speed of light in a vacuum is the same for all observers

Massive objects cause a distortion in space-time, which is felt as gravity

"Well, I think we know what to do but the how is the question. We have to go over the speed of light to go back in time"

"Agreed, that is the only way. However, that is too fast or we have to find a way to slow light down, make it go through something which has a higher refractive index, water or something else."

"Well, that is one way or we could find a way to warp space-time, create a wormhole, and go back in time"

"Ok let's build a wormhole"

It took them several weeks to convert the contraption they had built for time travel into the future, to traverse a wormhole, to go into the past. Funding cuts at the university meant they had to scrimp and use whatever they had to build the prototype wormhole.

They built a complex roller coaster ride for the gadget to simulate warped space-time. They tried to send a mouse with the prototype along with the camera. It finally worked after seven attempts. The four of them were elated.

Now they had to build the real thing. The lab was not going to cut it.

"Well Chen I guess now we have to go and get the SSC ready for the real action."

"Yes Arun, Yes"

The two of them were referring to the Superconducting Super Collider, Desertron, in Waxahachie, Texas, construction on which began in 1991 but was cancelled in 1993 because of funding issues. Thankfully, now because of their and other scien-

tific experiments, Rice and MIT had joint owner-
ship of the project and site.

Coordinates 32.2359° N, 96.5050° W

They spent the next several months, almost the entire summer in building a complex roller coaster ride. They also began designing a spherical ball, which they nicknamed Kadur, with enough room to hold seven people, which could traverse the wormhole.

The Desertron SSC was originally built as a particle accelerator complex however; scientists have been finding creative usage of it. There is a lot you can do when you have a 54-mile tunnel with high energy to play with. Light speed or close to light speed, experiments were routine.

They sent Kadur on many unmanned runs over the roller coaster rails. The idea was to use very high electromagnetic force to move Kadur over the rails. Kadur was never sitting on the rails except when stationary but mostly travelling at light speeds hovering over the rails, going up, down, sideways simulating warped space-time. Kadur came back with pictures of the past, which was not where they wanted to be, so adjustments and more adjustments were made to hit the right location and year.

One of the many runs took Kadur back to the dinosaur era, which was breathtaking.

They had to make other changes too. They had to change the external material coating of Kadur to use a polymer composite, which could resist the wear and tear of light-speed travel challenges.

Finally, Kadur was ready for time travel.

"One of us will have to stay back to man this device. It has to be either Chen or me"

"Well how do we decide that?" Chen did badly want to go. This was the past, that he did not know and he always had a desire to know everything.

"We flip a coin, Heads I win tails you win" Arun took out a coin and tossed it. The four peered onto the ground to see who won. It was heads.

"Sorry buddy" Arun said as he picked up the coin from the floor.

"Shit you always win when we flip a coin. You are so damn lucky."

"Sorry again bud" Arun smiled inwardly with the knowledge that this coin had heads on either side. "Ok let's get inside one at a time."

Arron went in first. Luciella went in next and Arun went in last and locked the hatchet after him.

Chen waited until everyone in had put their seat belts on before pressing the controls to start Kadur and energizing it.

Kadur rose up on the rails as it picked up energy until it was about six inches off the rails. Chen checked the latitude and longitude of the coordinates Kadur would be traversing to and then pressed the controls to send Kadur to the past. The spherical ball was gone in a flash, a ball of fire.

Coordinates - 28°32'23"N, 33°58'24"E

The three of them were transported to very close to where Moses Aaron Hur and Miriam were sleeping that night. The entourage was on their way to the Promised Land and resting for the night after a long day of travel. The night was pitch black. The trio checked each other out and everyone was fine, all bones intact.

On the desert, at a distance they saw some tents that had been put up. The three of them slowly moved towards the tents careful not to make any noise. There were two larger tents, which looked very robustly built set apart. There were other tents as well, but a bit far and were shabby looking.

They reached one of the larger tents in which Moses and Aaron were sleeping. They slowly peeked inside. The two guys were fast asleep. Slowly they went inside. Arron shook Aaron. Aaron woke up rubbing his eyes. He reached for his rod instinctively.

"Who are you?"

"I am Arron. Are you Moses?"

"No I am Aaron. What are you doing here & what do you want?"

"It's a long story but we need to meet Moses"

Aaron looked at the three and could not place them. They did not look Egyptian, Syrian or anyone that he had come across in his lifetime. They were dressed funny too, wearing clothes made of material, which he had never seen. He looked at them suspiciously.

"Do you come in peace or war?"

"Peace. We have come from very far; from the future. We are here to learn about the commandments. What was the context it was written in and we are hoping it will help us solve some of the burning questions all of us here have."

"Ok just read page 28 to page 38 of this book or thereabouts and you shall have you answers"

The three picked up the book and started reading the pages.

"Oh my God. The Commandments do not make any sense. It's a load of crap"

"Oh my God. So this is what happened and people have been thinking that these are the words of God"

"Lies, Lies all Lies" A visibly irritated Arron picked up the book and started beating up Aaron on the head with it, repeatedly.

All the commotion woke up Moses and even bothered Hur and Miriam in the other tent where they have been copulating all night long.

Moses rubbed his eyes "Who are these people"

"I don't know Moses. They said they are from the future and come in peace but then this guy beat me up with a book because we made up the commandments"

Just then, Miriam and Hur arrived.

Arun's eyes popped out of their sockets when he saw the newcomers especially Miriam. Her firm right breast was popping out over her clothes. Luciella mouth was wide open as she stared at Hur's crotch; his penis was up for public display. Both of them became acutely aware of the focus of Arun and Luciella and quickly adjusted their clothes to look more modest.

"Well we have to find answers to our questions. Real answers not make believe ones. Obviously, these made up commandments are not our answer. We have to find the person who gave you the commandments."

"God or someone important gave me the original commandments"

"Well then we have to find this person. Where were you given the commandments?"

"Well I can probably take you there."

"Wait a minute Moses. Remember last time what happened. You got lost, got very lucky, and found the place. Let us think of an alternate approach"

Aaron thought for a second and said, "I got it. Moses we will need to use our rods"

Aaron and Moses took out their rod and shaft respectively, and concentrated. They touched the tip of their rod and shaft. It began to glow brighter and brighter and then there was blinding white light and the brilliance and dazzle made them move back. Just as quickly, the glow came, it was gone.

On the ground between the two men was a papyrus with a message. Miriam picked it up and read it. It said

"Same place where I gave you the tablets. Make sure to follow the yellow brick road. You get a 30-minute window and yes, I will

tell you what the original commandments were. Meet me there tomorrow."

"Oh Well" Aaron sighed. Everyone else was awestruck; it was so easy to contact God. Finally Arron spoke, "This is great. Let's get a list of questions that we want to ask God or this important person."

The seven of them started thinking through the questions late into the night. There was lot of thought put into the questions to be asked.

Allowing for 2 minutes to answer each question, 14/15 questions were all they could possibly fit in the 30 minutes. That was not much and what if there were follow up questions. They had to take a hatchet and not a scalpel to reduce the number of questions but it was clear that they were going to go over time however much they planned and if they wanted the meeting to be effective.

Many questions were considered but left out as they were thought to be not relevant or not important enough.

Some of the questions considered were:

What is Kim Kardashian going to do next and what is going to happen in her family?

81

What is happening in the next episode of the Game of thrones and Big Bang theory?

Is Lente Loco ever going to come back? Where can I see the reruns?

Who is going to win the NASCAR this year?

Who is going to win the NFL championship this year?

Who is going to win the NBA and WNBA championship this year?

Who is going to win the MLB this year?

What are the next Powerball & Mega Million winning numbers?

Am I going to win the lotto?

What is the best pickup line to impress chicks and dudes?

Why do some plants eat insects?

Does a black cat bring bad luck?

Should I sign up for health insurance, Obamacare? Should I buy any insurance for that matter, home, car etc?

Are UFOs for real?

Do Ghosts and Goblins exist?

How to understand who is a friend and who is not?

Is there a way to make the traffic signal be green always whichever road I am travelling?

Will the perpetual crisis in the Middle East ever end?

Is Gambling a sin?

Is smoking weed a sin?

Is paper money ever going to be replaced completely?

Where did Liam hide his playboy collections?

It was almost morning before the seven concluded on the questions to ask God or someone important.

Coordinates - 28°32'23"N, 33°58'24"E

With barely an hour or two of sleep, they left in search of the yellow brick road after having a hearty breakfast of Shakshuka.

Hur prepared breakfast for everyone using a cast iron pan over a clay oven. Though the ingredients were the same, eggs, tomatoes, hot peppers and onions he tailored it to each person's taste and spice tolerance. For Arron he fully fried the egg, as he could not tolerate poached eggs. For Aaron he added some potatoes. Moses, Arun, and Luciella asked for some extra onions. For Miriam he added extra paprika and cumin.

The food was delicious. Every bit of bread was used to mop up the delicious sauce. No one left a drop of sauce or bread on his or her plate. Moses ate the most.

Aaron Moses and Miriam got dressed in their finest. Hur however still wore his work overalls. He never knew when he would be called for work so he liked to be always prepared. They were going to meet someone important or God and treated this no different from Sunday Church or Saturday Synagogue. The only thing that was unclear was whether the service they were going to could be compared to the morning Shacharit, afternoon Micha or evening Maariv or havdalah prayer service and if they were appropriately dressed.

The other three did not have any option as they continued to wear what they time travelled in, jeans and t-shirt.

Moses was the only one amongst all of them that prayed three times a day with a religious rigor, which was amazing, only to be one-upped by Arun's mom doing it five times a day. But, does it really matter!

They were relying on Moses to find the beginnings of the yellow brick road. The seven of them walked for three hours with no yellow brick road in sight. They were getting weary. Everyone was annoyed with Moses. He would see a path and then with supreme confidence lead everyone to it and it would end up in a dead-end.

Suddenly Luciella had an idea. She was reminded of an old movie she had watched about the silly wizard of oh wowZ.

"Look all we have to do is find the munchkin people and they should be able to direct us." She said excitedly.

"Munchkin people? There are no munchkin people." Moses said

"Do you mean the Munkacs People?" Hur asked

"I guess so" Luciella shrugged.

"The Munkacs," Arun said rhetorically, "are a hasidec sect within Haredi Judaism. Rabbi Shloma Spira founded it. Now most of them are in Brooklyn, New York"

"I don't know about Brooklyn but they live over there, beyond those hills." Hur pointed to some hills a little distance away.

Arun was scratching his head. As far as he knew, the Munkacs belonged to the town of Munkacs, a Hungarian town that was now in Mukachevo in Ukraine.

Then he realized it was possible to have a city named the same in two different countries. He was reminded of cities in the real England and cities in New England with similar names like Manchester, New London, Stratford, and Windsor.

"You know I just remembered something" Aaron spoke excitedly. "Munkacland has the walking tree"

"A walking tree?"

"Yes a walking and talking tree. So, an interesting tree walks around and bears different fruits in each of its branches. On one branch, you could find apples, on another branch oranges, mangoes, or bananas. In addition, every week the fruits on the branches change. Also, you can have a conversation with her."

"Really?" Luciella was excited.

"Yes"

It took them an hour to get over the hills and sure enough at the top of the hill, was one of the most colorful of cities. It certainly looked very advanced for the times. A board at the city limits said Munkacland, population 257. Excited they entered the city.

They saw a short, potbellied dignified man wearing glasses and a hat in a bright red coat and approached him.

"Sir, do you know where the yellow brick road is."

"Are you looking to meet someone important or God?"

"Yes" Aaron said hesitantly

"You must be Moses," the man said excitedly.

"No I am not. He is" Aaron said pointing to Moses.

The man went over and kissed Moses's hand tears flowing down his cheeks. "Melinda, the good witch told us about you, that you will come here with others. I am Abba, the mayor of Munkacland and I insist that you have lunch with us"

The others agreed. It was noontime and they were getting hungry.

Just then, they heard a whistle and true to what they had heard, a tree came walking by whistling. The tree did have a bit of a swagger in her walk and she was full of wonderful different exotic fruits on each branch. She stopped when she saw them.

"Hi there. Welcome to Munkacland? My name is Sharak Alon" She said cheerfully "Do you want a fruit? It's far better than eating fries or a burger."

Nobody did but they all thanked her after asking her some questions about the names of the exotic fruits on her branches.

Abba led them to a colorful house splashed with all the colors of the rainbow, where his wife Adina greeted them. Adina was short and round and a very pleasant person with a bright smile which lit up the world. She wore a bright blue dress with yellow flowers on them.

"Welcome to our humble home" She led them to the dining table where a feast awaited them. It almost seemed like they were expecting them and had prepared the meal just for them.

What they did not know was that the mayor, his wife was very large hearted, and he had a habit of getting a few folks over for every meal from all over town. They were not very rich but their hearts were full of love and made of gold.

The Mayor was also a real leader. He cared for his people and lead through his heart. He wanted well for his people. He was open to altruistic support. He however resisted any money from unscrupulous businesses or superpacs to run his city that typically have their own agenda to push, a pipeline here a contract there!

The people in his city were truly free and happy. The mayor and his wife gave everything they had to the poor and needy and urged others to do so too.

Adina was like a mother hen, as she made sure everyone had a full meal. She was serving the food and kept insisting people have more, in a very sweet manner, that you could not refuse.

The amount of food on the table could feed an army. She had the traditional food from the region matzoh ball soup, savory kugel, borekas, bazargan, and cholent. For desert, she made the traditional Matzo. She also had baklava, khazandibi, and Künefe. Everyone ate to their heart content especially Mo. Nobody could move for almost ten minutes after they finished eating.

They were in food coma. Arun ate everything except the Künefe.

Miriam tried to prevent Mo from overeating. Mo had a habit of eating like a pig but that was not the issue. He was a public embarrassment after he ate, as he would fart continuously after that. Usually it was only the sound but sometimes the smell would be unbearable.

Back when in Egypt the skill of his was put to good use. He was called on to torture prisoners who were crucified. They would feed him a diet of oatmeal, broccoli, and garlic for a day to power him into action. The following day they would let him lose on the prisoners. The crucified prisoners would try to cover their noses but their hands were tied. There were few survivors from those torture sessions and torture methods.

After they finished their meal, they thanked Abba and Adina and lounged in the verandah talking and watching people on the street.

Luciella asked Abba "Do you by any chance have the crystal ball?"

"I have several crystal balls, which one?"

"The one that professor Marmalade used"

"Don't know who that is but I have one which was once used by the priests of Isis and Osiris in the land of the Pharaohs. Follow me, I'll show you."

"Ok" Luciella jumped up excited from her chair.

Abba took her inside and showed her the crystal ball. It was beautiful and magical. She peered into it. It had gone dark.

"Do you use it?"

"No but I hear it has magical powers and you can see the past and future with that. There was a man here once, in a travelling wagon. I forget his name but he knew how to use it but he left soon. He said something about having to leave to meet the crown heads of Europe. He said he was from the land of *E pluribus unum*"

"Okay" Luciella thought that sounds so like Professor Marmalade.

"Shall we go back now to be with the others?"

"Sure"

They went back to the verandah and sat down. While they sat there and chitchatted the Rock 'n Roll guild of five members and Cuban Cigar only league of three members stopped by to meet them.

The Rock 'n Roll guild first set stage and after 5 minutes of testing the acoustics, they let go on the audience with their blaring music. When they sang, it sounded more like yelling and when they danced, you could argue it was mostly jumping around like monkeys. They were certainly entertaining because once they got into the groove everyone was rocking their bodies back and forth synchronizing with the music. At the end of their performance, they presented each of the visitors with a hand-autographed picture.

Moved by all the excitement of the moment Luciella bared her breast and the lead guitarist of the guild autographed his name across her chest. He told her that they were going on tour and asked her if she would like to join them but she declined.

The Cuban Cigar only league huffed and they puffed as they danced the Bolero and at the end of their dance routine, they gave each of the visitors a hug and a cigar as a memento.

The residents of the town came by one by one young and old, man and woman, boy and girl to meet them. They were a colorful, cheerful lot and they sang, danced, and thanked them for coming by. Sharak Alon came as well and thanked them for coming. She gave each of them a hug and a fruit.

The whole experience was very touching and the visitors did not want to leave. Love is a powerful force and difficult to resist. It pulls at your heart and at times can leave you with an empty sinking feeling deep down in your gut when it is time to leave. Every one of them felt that. However, they had to go. They had a mission to accomplish.

"Abba I think we have to leave. Can you show us to the yellow brick road?" Moses asked with a heavy heart.

"Follow me" Abba gave a deep sigh.

Abba took them behind a huge barn behind his house where there was a well-manicured lawn. You could see Mt Sinai behind it. He walked over the grass until he reached a point. The others followed him.

Back at the house, Adina was sobbing uncontrol lably. She loved it when people came but was heartbroken when they left. Deeply emotional people are like that and unfortunately, the world treats them like shit.

"Here you go," he said pointed to a clearing where there was a paved walkway painted in yellow. The walkway winded itself into the mountain of Sinai.

"Can I ask you a favor before you go?"

"Sure"

"When you meet God or someone important can you ask that the people in Munkacland remain happy forever?"

"You mean healthy, wealthy, and wise"

"Just happy I think. We don't need much wealth; we have enough of it to live. Once you chase that you can never have enough of it. I think we could be happy if we were healthy because healthcare is getting expensive and being healthy could make some of us happy. Wise yes we could do with more books. We don't have enough. Yes healthy and wise would be good as well"

"Done, we will put in the word"

They thanked Abba and started walking the path.

They chit chatted as they walked and would occasionally burst into songs and the munkacs who were tilling the soil on the side of the road joined in and egged them on. Some of the munkacs who came from Russia and other foreign lands sang the same song in their languages. The sky was filled with music and love. The flowers and trees swayed to the music.

O what a wonderful land
The land that is Munkacland
The land with the whistling tree

The land where everybody is happy
And free [2]

Rock'n Roll
Cuban Cigar
Abba Adina
Sharak Alon
Whistling tree
Can't you see?
Happy People
Definitely [2]

Hur disappeared enroute on the yellow brick road and started picking up some very colorful wild flowers and bulrushes he noticed. He cut the stem of the bulrushes to size to match the size of the flower stem and made two bunches and tied them up with strands of grass. They looked very pretty. He ran back and handed one to Luciella and one to Miriam. Both the girls gave him a kiss on either cheek.

Miriam asked Arun why he had such an unusual name. Arun explained to her that though he was born in the USA his parents were from the southern part of India and the name reflected the town, city that he was born in or been to. In addition, the fathers and mothers name could be in the name including the town, city they were born or been to. His name was his DNA fingerprint.

"So Taj Mahal is a place?"

"No that's my mother's name; she is Muslim and a descendant of Mumtaz Mahal, wife of Shah Jahan who built the Taj Mahal. My dad was a Hindu though and I am too. Kerela, Cochin are places though."

"Oh" she said wondering what strange people and stranger names.

"Miriam do you know what nunatak and scherenschnitte mean?"

"No"

"How about feuilleton and stichomythia?

"No"

"Well these were some of the words I had to spell when I won the national spelling bee contest. I was six years old then. At that time, I had just memorized the words. It's only recently that I took some time to understand what they mean."

"Oh" Miriam was impressed.

"Nunatak is an exposed rocky edge, not covered by snow within a glacier. Scherenschnitte is the art of paper cutting design. Stichomythia is a verse drama of sequence of single alternating lines given to alternating characters. Feuilleton is an install-ment of a serial story printed in one part of a newspaper." Arun bragged.

"Oh" Miriam exclaimed, impressed but not fully understanding.

"Can I ask you a question that has been bothering me?"

"I guess"

"How many plagues were there? Were there really ten?"

"No, there were seven. There was the pollution of the lakes, which led to the plague of frogs, mil-lions of them invading our homes. Then there was the plague of the locusts, which wiped away our crops. There was the plague of the diseased livestock. Soon after, there was one where people had boils, skin eruptions unexpectedly. Then there was the plague of thunderstorm of hail and fire followed by a plague of flies. The worst was the plague of the lice as that affected the royal family and gave the Pharaoh fodder to kick us out and you can add the fact that my brother killed an Egyptian."

"Okay, thank you. That was very informative. I will take that back and have history rewritten. You love your brother a lot don't you?"

"Yes and I love you too. You are both my younger brothers and I won't let harm come either of your ways" Miriam gave him a tight hug and a peck on his cheeks.

Miriam quickly doubled up her steps to where Luciella was walking next to Hur and the three of them chitchatted.

It took them a couple of hours to get to the same place where Moses had received the commandments.

Coordinates - 28°32'23"N, 33°58'24"E

"We're here, where are you" Moses shouted trying to get God's or someone important's attention.

There in the mountains by the stream a miracle happened. Something similar to last time, a faint white glow with a bluish tinge appeared from nowhere grew very large but this time from the blinding light emerged someone who looked important and Goddish.

The silhouette started walking towards them and everyone gasped once the silhouette was recognizable. Wait a minute! God was black and a woman!

She was beautiful. She had long black hair which came down to her waist, an hourglass figure, a beautiful smile with perfectly white teeth. She was perfect and pleasing in every way and everyone was awestruck. She was wearing an elegant off shoulder figure hugging white gown. She did not have too much jewelry on her but what she had on was classy. She did not have an ounce of extra fat on her body and she wore sexy stilettos. She definitely did not look like yo' mama.

"Accho…Hi there" God spoke in a nasal voice as she sneezed "Sorry about this. I have a bad cold"

Everyone was curious. How could God catch a cold?

"I know what you are thinking. Yes, we have affirmative action at our workplace. I have been travelling, responding to prayers from space enthusiasts and engineers at the John Hopkins University who goofed up their trajectory calculations, so I was making major adjustment to the travel path of New Horizons so it could take good pictures of Pluto. That would explain the cold. The kuiper belt and that part of space are cold even for me." She sneezed again.

"Now I know you are here for the actual commandments and I will tell you what they are when we are done but I believe you also have a few questions. So shoot we don't have too much time."

Luciella asked the first question.
"How are you organized and how do you operate?"

"We run no different than a large corporation. We run no different from the IBMs of the world. We have a board of seven and one amongst us on a rotating basis becomes Chairman or God for a finite amount of time. So for the next seven years, seven months and seven days I get to be God. Of course, there are demigods having territories that they manage for efficient functioning of the universe. We have annual conferences and have adhoc meetings as well. We try to work as a cohesive unit."

"We are also funded very well and we get funds from various religious organizations in cash and kind. We have layoff too, 10% every year, usually for those who cannot get 10 % from the constituents they serve. We take our mandate seriously and have to function like a very well oiled machinery"

Miriam went next.
"How does it feel to be God and having all the powers? How often do people call you to get their wish granted?"

"You think it is easy to be God! Earth and there are a few others from where we get incessant calls, some easy and some hard to fulfill requests. It is not funny the number of calls we get from this planet though. From the seemingly innocuous requests of getting passing grades to more profound ones of save my child, we get more than a trillion requests per second just from human beings on earth. It is not easy to answer each call however we try to do our best."

"When we initially started this, we planned everything to play out in auto mode with no manual intervention. We followed the SDLC, the software delivery life cycle process and went through lab, development, QA, stress, pre-prod, and then production to ensure everything was working properly without any glitches."

"For the solar system, we made the planets revolve around the sun on a schedule. For the earth, we planned the sunrises and sunset, cycle of life for all living beings but then man came and messed up everything. They created imbalance in the eco system we had so carefully set up. That was the bug if you will in our program."

"Is there life on other planets?"

"Yes, Life as in human-like life on many planets and life in general on a much larger number of planets"

"Why was the world created and how will it end?"

"Oh God! The answer will take up several hours and certainly eat up the time we have allocated here. Set up a meeting with more time if you really want this question answered. Next question please"

Miriam wondered if you could exclaim at yourself, perhaps only if you are God she thought.

"What is your position on Sex?"

"Moderation is important. Missionary is good but it is ok to try other positions. Since the primary purpose is so that the seed, I mean the semen stays in; woman on top may not be a good idea but could be ok for the secondary purpose, fun. In addition, I do not condone doggy style. I can get into details on why but does that answer your question?"

"No I meant as in is sex between two men or two women wrong? Are 3-somes, orgies, swinging, and zoophilia ok? What is your opinion about agalmatophilia, nantaimori, nyotaimori, salirophilia, BDSM ? Is it ok to indulge in that or is that off limits?"

"I plead the fifth"

"Is it a sin to watch porn?" Arun asked sincerely

"It depends. Soft porn is ok. Hard core porn is not."

"And Masturbating"

"Two to three times a week is enough. You need to stop your daily adventures young man. You could develop a sore." God had a twinkle in her eye as she spoke to Arun and then turned and smiled at Luciella.

Luciella sheepishly made a circle with her toes in the sand. She knew that God knew that she was pleasuring herself upwards of seven times a day. Back of her mind, she knew she was overdoing it but she felt she could not help it.

"So what do you think of the oldest profession in the world?"

"It's hard work. Competition is tough."

"What diet should we follow? Is it a sin to eat meat? Killing pigs, cows, and other animals to feed ourselves? Should food be kosher only?"

"I thought I made sure there was abundance of fruits and vegetables on earth. In addition, I thought there was an abundance of milk and honey. I guess if man wants to eat meat what can I say. If you want to be a lion or an animal, that eats other animals, do so. I will tell you this though if you want to evolve you will need to moderate what you eat. If you have to eat meat make sure you eat it in moderation especially red meat. Also food does not need to be kosher only"

"Do you have an email address?"

"Yes ohmygod@ncipb.com. You can also use someone.important@ncipb.com"

"Who is hosting your mail server?"

"godaddy"

"How much are you paying for that?"

"God, you don't have to answer that. Arun that question is irrelevant."

"Well I was only trying to find out if God got a better deal than I did for mail hosting service. I already have a good deal on my cable connection. I always feel that I don't get the best deal when I go looking for one, be it when I try to buy a car, rent an apartment, or anything. I think it is my brown skin. Racial profiling I tell you."

Arron stared down hard at Arun. God was shaking her head.

Arron was getting increasingly worried that people were not playing by the rules and asking questions that were off the agreed to list. As a football player, he understood the value of order and discipline and rules unlike his friends. Particularly Luciella was very disorderly. He remembered the times he visited her room when they were lovers. He had to climb a tree to get in through the window to her room on the second floor of her father's house.

He then had to navigate a maze of books, magazines, bra, and panties to get to her bed to make out with her. He also remembered the few times he slipped from a branch while trying to get to her room and falling down and her father coming out with a shotgun, firing in the air, thinking it was an intruder. Love is crazy he thought.

Luciella question to God brought him back from his reverie.

"Do you have to shave?"

"Of course I do. To look pretty all of us do."

"I would have never guessed that from your flawless skin"

"Thank you" God then proceeded to show them her underarm and pulled up her gown considerably to show them her legs. They were flawless and smooth and there was not a single hair follicle on either her underarm or legs.

"Good God! You have fabulous legs!" exclaimed Arun, his jaw dropping. Except for Arron, the others were too mesmerized to say anything coherent though Moses did make a feeble attempt.

"Thanks" God was blushing. It appeared that even God was not inure to compliments. Even God liked to hear a nice thing or two occasionally, even if it was as shallow as being complimented on how she looked.

Arron was shaking his head. This was so off topic and so not the reason they had travelled so far.

"So how do you do it? Laser hair removal, razor, tweezers, waxing, or electrolysis?"

"Herbs. I use herbs"

The men listened intently as well. Some of them had been trying to get a clean-shaven chest and back, where the hair did not grow back, and had been unsuccessful until now. This information was good.

"Is there anything you can do for me? Is there a cure for baldness?" Moses asked.

"Of course and again herbs. I will send you the recipe to the concoction. You will need to apply it to your scalp once a fortnight for one year and after that you will never have a baldness problem again."

"Is there a price tag?"

"$9.99 + Shipping and handling for each product. You can buy both for $14.99. We take Master-Card, Visa. Recently we added PayPal as well. Look God Inc is a not for profit organization but research needs funding. We had and have to hire top talents. It took a while to figure out the herbs to induce and prevent balding. By the way, if you refer a friend you get a 10 % discount on your next purchase and your friend a 5 % discount. Just make sure your friend refers your name when making the purchase"

Moses was happy. Part of the reason he had not been getting dates, he thought, was because he was bald and now finally he had a solution that would grow back his hair and get him those dates. Little did he know that some women like bald men but what they cannot stand are men who are not confident, stutter, and stammer. Some like rich bald men even more and would even waive the stuttering and stammering consideration, in fact go as far as waiving all considerations.

"Do you wear a bra?" Luciella was curious

"Yes even Gods need support."

"What brand?"

"Victoria's secret of course. Same as what is worn by all our angels." She turned towards Arun anticipating his question "It's a 36 C push up bra."

"Can we move on to more important questions" Aaron interjected. "What is your role in scientific finding?"

"None. I do not take credit for any. I did create humans though and gave them a brain and an environment where they can exercise that"

"Is everyone created equal and if not why not? Why is there disparity between the haves and the have not's, the rich and the poor?"

"That was the initial idea, like I said the idea was process and automation in creating the worlds. Humans, they are constantly trying to game the system and any system that you try to constantly game at some point or other will give in and will not work. When you affect the environment, it will affect you too. Works both ways. We have to work to fix that. It will take some time but the deep divide between the rich and poor will end. I promise you that."

"Why are some people born rich and others poor?"

"This is where the karmic effects come to play."

"Why is life so unfair? Why is there so much sorrow and issues? Why give cancer to a baby or a child? Why do good people have to live a life of poverty while assholes flourish?"

"I'm sorry. I have not been able to save many. I have not been able to get there and take action in time. Babies with cancer, I am so sorry" God wiped a tear. "I do want good things to happen in this world I created. As far as the assholes let me take that back to the board."

"What about the corrupt, inept leaders, CEOs, popes, imams, rabbis, gurus, politicians, lawyers, judges, and generally bad people all around? Why do you put the bad, inept ones in a position of power?"

"I don't. They game the system and move up and then get their cronies around them but let me take that back to the board and see if we can collectively think of something. I did not realize things were so bad and again I am sorry. This will need manual intervention"

"Well then why is their justice delayed whereas murderers, thieves get their justice handed out to them immediately?"

"Yes I agree there is a problem here. It appears money, influence is pretty much tilting the balance, and creating inequality and the root cause seems to be greed. I can only say we are overwhelmed right now with the things we have to fix but another item that I will take back to the board to discuss and address. Right now, we are working in a reactive mode and putting in tactical fixes. We definitely need to step back and take a more strategic approach"

"Why do people die and what happens next?"

"I think this is a loaded question. Set up some more time with me, the time we have here is not enough. However in short the reason each person dies is unique and so is what happens next."

"Where do thoughts originate from? Do you have anything to do with it? Can one person have his or her thoughts influence another without the normal channel of communication like speech?"

"Thoughts originate from the mind. The drivers are many. You see something and think of some thing similar or something related. I think too and send those thoughts out, as do some accomplished thinkers who can channelize their thoughts. A part of thoughts in your dream or even when you are awake is that. You catch a glimpse of other people's thought that you are attune to, somewhat like a radio channel. You filter those in and others you filter out. However to receive those thoughts you need to silence your mind"

"So yes, there is subtle influence. There is an extreme case where the influence is no longer subtle and some people have harnessed the power to do so. They can target their thoughts to a person or a group and influence them to a point they take over them temporarily. When it is for good I don't mind, when for bad which is rare, I step in. Some people have the power of telekinesis. I worry about them"

"My humanities professor keeps saying seven words that can change your life *you can if you think you can*. Is that true or is everything predetermined?"

"Mostly pre-determined, there is room for some minor modifications to the general course of life but not much. If you want something very bad, you will get it eventually but by the time you get it you may not want it as much. So careful on what you think you want"

"Why are there so many religions?"

"Religion is big for me. That is how we sustain ourselves. That is what funds us and we believe in the concept of different strokes for different folks. Not one religious doctrine fits all"

"What is your take on abortion?"

"It has been a matter of much debate even at the board. We are taking this very seriously. Life is important but trying to determine exactly when life begins is a questionable item. We do not want to brush this in one stroke and want to look at the nuances in the life of a prenatal human and then there is the issue of women rights. It is a complicated subject and there is some work to be done to come up with a solution that works for everyone and is fair to everyone"

"Why did you bring about the concept of marriage?"

"No I did not. You did. Marriages are made on earth not heaven."

"Well at least do you have an opinion? Is it ok for men to marry men and women to marry women?

"Marriage is an institution created on earth. As far as my opinion, I do not see a problem. I guess someone had the idea to create this institution to bring controls in society and to prevent people from copulating randomly with others and it caught on across civilizations."

"It then evolved into creating order and the family became the basic unit of society. Governments then brought into the concept and very soon, corporations and the legal entities were created around the concept to support the family."

"Today financials, property rights are created such so that it stays within the family. So what you are

113

really asking is whether changing the concept of family to include same sex couples is ok? I think it is ok. Additionally extending the rights to family, someone's partner should get their money and property when either one dies. I am not opposed to it. In case they want to bring up kids I am not opposed to that either."

"Is there a heaven?"

"No. I am sorry when I said that before when I was talking of marriages, it was just a figure of speech"

"So what happens when we die?"

"You are dead."

"So no afterlife or reincarnation, the stuff we read about and are told about?"

"Well there was, but we looked at it and with the population explosion that happened with that approach, we slowed it down. So, earlier there were people being born with new souls and souls, which had reincarnated. You get the idea. It is a tactical solution we have now, but we are working on a strategic solution. We are also very worried about the change in China's one child policy. This is what happens when people fuck around too much."

"What about hell. Is there a hell?"

"Hell no. I mean no there is no hell. So let me explain, earlier when a person died, the body perished and got broken down by the elements until it was one with nature, we took the soul and put it into a new born. So now, we do not do that anymore all the time. We store the souls. They are cryogenically frozen as a figure of speech. If you want to call that hell that would be it"

"So where do bad people go?"

"Same place good people go. All souls are currently cryogenically frozen. I am not saying that things won't change but that is how things are right now"

"So where are the souls frozen?"

"Mars."

"Oh this sounds so like a prison system we have, Guantanamo. We have good and bad souls over there and the government has been trying to figure out what to do for many years now. Sometimes I feel bad for the good souls who went there when they were boys and are now grown men. Some died in that prison. Anyways so that's what we are going to find when we go to Mars" Luciella quipped.

"Yes and some water." God sighed. Luciella's comment was not lost on her and she cried on the inside. What kind of assholes was allowed to lead countries in the name of democracy she thought while God Inc was a silent bystander while all this happened?

"What about conscience? Is it part of the soul?"

"Yes, there is the person made of flesh and there is a subtler piece, the soul, which makes the person tick. The conscience is part of the person that helps people make choices that are right for them. "

"Can two souls merge?"

"Yes, have you heard of love? It happens when two souls love. When two souls love, they merge"

"Can you tell us how you became a God and also how does one become a demigod"

God took a deep breath and then started.
"Ok Gods, demigods are really evolved souls. Now note that not all the religions in the world have it right but a few do. Eventually they all will get to the truth as long as they keep an open mind. Anyways we are evolved souls and have been able to get out of the cycle of life and death"

"Oh so you are not real?"

"It depends on your definition of real. Our souls have been purified by going through the school of many lives."

"So you were human once?"

"Yes."

"Can you tell us what you were before getting the big God promotion?"

"Well I was Marie Curie last before I got the big promotion if you will"

"Marie Curie the scientist" Arun exclaimed, "She is my hero. She won two Nobel prizes." He ran over to God and hugged her tightly. God smiled. She actually was also the first person to get it twice and one of the few who got it for physics and chemistry.

"I was also Queen Isabella of Spain. I made a lot of mistakes but I was really sorry for what I did and tried to address that then and in many successive births"

Everyone stared at her hard. God's head was hung in shame. The atrocities she as Isabella the catholic committed in the name of purifying the religion were numerous. The inquisitions mainly targeting the Jews and Muslims converts are well documented in history books.

"I also sent Christopher Columbus to the Americas," She said sheepishly.

Everyone stared even harder. Miriam changed the subject.

"Why is there so much death and destruction in the world? Why are there earthquakes, tsunamis and other natural calamities?

"It is the natural checks and balance we have put to run the place on auto-pilot to maintain balance, and to control the population explosion."

"So does that make you a bad God or a good God? There are destructions and killings on one hand and creation on the other. I cannot forget the Tsunamis in Japan and Phuket, Thailand. Nor the earthquakes in Pakistan, Haiti. Katrina, Sandy. The list is long"

"Oh! Sometimes I feel I am not a God at all. By the way, you don't have to call me God, just somebody important. All I can say is we are striving to strike a balance. Not every action we take will benefit all; this is no different from what happens in large corporations. For profitability sometime, you have to fire old farts and hire new blood. I'll use the same analogy for the earth where there is destruction and creation occurring simultaneously."

Luciella was offended to hear that. Her dad was not a fart. A hard working postal worker, they first reduced his hours and then laid him off. He tried to find work without luck and finally gave up and retired.

Nobody said it for fear of an age discrimination lawsuit but age was not on his side. Businesses are more willing to hire young clueless people rather than experienced mature healthy ones who know what they are doing.

These days he did odd handyman jobs and when not doing any of that, could be found on his porch with a beer, smoking a pipe and brooding about life. Also once a week for an hour, he volunteered to teach inner-city kids in an afterschool program. He was not a terribly successful man but he did not want the same for his kids and also kids in his community. He was very proud of his children especially Luciella. He missed his wife and kids terribly. He sometimes found solace in the arms of Crystal at the local cabaret, Wispers.

"Why is someone created a man, but really is a woman? Why are there people created who are mentally inept and their actions incoherent?"

"Manufacturing defect. Remember we are creating millions of people so some anomalies are expected. It is not a perfect system and we have tried to fix it but that has caused more problems. We also have to find out if we would like to leave the anomalies in place. Another thing to take back to the board."

"Are there Karmic effects and what are the time frames?"

"Yes there are karmic effects. You do something good today; you will get a just return sometime later. The same holds true for doing something bad. We came up with a rate card. It has timelines on when you get something for doing something. Send me an email and I will send you the rate card. I do want to tell you this is not implemented to the letter because of inefficiencies of implementation."

"An example of good karmic effects is you study for four years at a college and at the end of it you will get a job. Sometimes you may have to wait a few more months up to eight months. Another example is when you help an old man or woman cross the street, they will bless you immediately, and that goes towards your life plan, rather funds your life 401k, and then you get a windfall every five, ten years later on in life. Something really awesome happens in your life. Write to me and I will tell you more."

"How do you go about implementing the rewards or punishments from the karmic effects?"

"Judges, lawyers in most cases. Governmental organizations in some cases. Random people in other cases. So in the instance of a crime committed by a person there is the judicial system handing down the punishment. In a place where that does not exist, people meet out punishment. In the case of good done by you, an altruistic deed like preventing someone from committing suicide and others the favor will be returned by some other person in your time of need or it could go into your life 401k plan."

"We also have started using drones to be more efficient and are prototyping a program. There have been some successes but many failures. Earlier we had a process of meting out justice manually and in specific cases; we sent a bolt of lightning or made a boat capsize to take out a specific person. Our plan with the invisible drones is to automatically track what exactly is happening around the universe and take action when there is crime. The action could be a bolt of lightning hitting the perpetrator of the crime."

"What kind of failures have you run into?"

"Well several but one was similar to the doctors without borders hospital bombing. There was some misunderstanding and a bolt of lightning that was sent down destroyed several orphanages and its residents instead of taking down the ISIS commanders. Another time we shot down a plane with hundreds on board."

"What is your take on the death penalty? Should it stay or go away?"

"Well, I think it should be an option however to argue for that, is a challenge in these times. There have been too many times that things have gone bad. Innocent people have been framed because of how the Jury system meted out justice and people had to pay with their lives, however there are some really bad people whose souls need cleansing. One option I have been thinking, using the current judicial system is give them life sentences and put them on a treadmill 8 hours a day and harness that energy to power the prison system and also giving back to the grid. So I would like to keep the death penalty option with some modifications in the judicial system however the recourse to the death penalty should be a last step."

"You mean reserve it for seriously bad people like serial killers, serial rapists, people who commit ghastly crimes?"

"Exactly. I am not sure how life imprisonment will help here. There is no possibility that these people will change or want to change so why waste everyone's time."

"Why does one have a desire to have sex?"

"This is by design to procreate. Just like, you feel hungry for food. Sex is for the sustenance of the human species"

"Why do people cheat on their partners?"

"That's a morality thing. Everyone has their own morals"

"So it is ok to cheat?"

"No it is not ok to cheat. If you want to cheat that is up to you but be prepared for the consequences. Morality is a big sustaining force for us and we will come after you at some point even though we may be overwhelmed and overworked here right now"

"Why did you do nothing when the child sex scandal at the church broke and other such atrocities at other religious places of worship?"

God was at a loss of words. "Sorry, we took action but it was delayed."

"What do you think about gun laws?"

"Inadequate and I will leave it at that"

"What about genocide, ethnic cleansing, and wars?"

"They should stop. People should live peacefully together. We have taken a hands off approach to that until now considering that checks and balances are in place. There is the UN and there is the Security Council to take action and get in front of international atrocities, same with wars. The international organizations should do their job and act quickly."

"Will we get to see the Promised Land?"

"I can't divulge that but don't accept all the prophesies and what the historians are saying. You are better off relying on what Anno Nomius has to say"

"Will I get to meet my mom and siblings?"

God sighed. "Even I can't tell child. I did not create the borders or create the immigration department and certainly not their backlog. All I can say is keep pressing on the politicians, maybe get a signed petition from all the people from your district, and give it to them to effect a change. Above all don't let them build walls between countries."

"How important are books. Should we believe what's in them?"

"Books are very important. Read them with an open mind and read lots of them. However the important thing is to believe in your own self and put to test what is written."

"So we should believe and follow the torah of the Jews, bible of the Christians, Koran of the Muslims, Gita of the Hindus and Popul Vuh of the Mayans?"

"Talk about double standards. Yesterday's technology is old today. How often does religion get an OS upgrade? Read them. Check them for validity in the current context and above all do not go about killing someone because you read it somewhere. Also remember even a good book will have flaws so just because you liked eight of the ten ideas, it does not mean the other two ideas are good or even right."

Aaron then conveyed the wishes of Abba and God approved his requests.

"Can you tell us what's in our future?"

"Well Moses you will be remembered and will become famous, more famous after your death. You Miriam will be famous amongst Jewish women. Hur you will most likely marry or be considered Miriam's adopted son. Aaron nobody will remember you even though you will have worked your ass off on various aspects of deliverance of the Jewish people from the land of the Pharaoh."

"You Arron will become a football star and later become a part-time football commentator once your head injuries leave you useless on the field. You will put your sports management degree to good use at the NFL."

"Luciella you will get a PhD, become a professor and later on will become very famous. If you want to marry Arron, you will need to work on building his trust."

"Arun you will be the youngest to receive two Nobel prizes in physics by age 30. The first you will get by 22 for time travel. You will get these awards jointly with Chen but you will be the youngest since you are a month younger than Chen"

"Ok I think our time is over. I have to leave"

"I had a personal question for you"

"Sure Arron" God certainly looked tired from answering all the questions. She looked at the others. They moved away to a distance to give Arron and God some privacy.

"So what is your question?"

"It's about my mom and sister and girlfriend's sexual escapades"

"Ok I know. However, consider this. You live in Mustang, Texas that has a population of 21. Eight of those living there are children and have not reached puberty. Six are women. That leaves seven men. Therefore, your mom slept with four men and your sister with three and that too over many years, almost 15 years for your mom and 7 years for your sister. Now is that very bad? Also, if you get technical and consider that there was no actual sexual intercourse and only fellatio in some cases the case is weak. Bill Clinton could not be impeached on these grounds if you remember."

Arron had not considered the facts but this gave him a renewed perspective, which made him feel good.

"As far as Luciella she is free spirited and exploring her sexuality but loves only you. She is curious and wants to learn about anything and everything. She is compassionate and loving. She will be president of your country one day I am telling you. Mark my word!"

Arron thanked God.

"Ok I have to leave" God told Arron and waved at the others at a distance. "Goodbye"

All of a sudden, the glow from which God had stepped out from re-appeared in the horizon and God spoke as she walked into it.

"Here are the commandments." She said and raised one hand and pointed to the sky.

The commandments started appearing before them etched in the skies. It was beautiful. The white cloud was forming sentences against the blue skies. Each sentence would stay for just so long so they could read it and then fade into the next sentence.

Be Good Do good and always do the right thing. When in doubt remove all noise and mental strife and ask the heart what the right thing to do is and you will get an answer. Listen to that.

Treat people well. You do not know where they are coming from, what they have gone through. Have compassion.

Be self-reliant and confident.

Be happy & thankful. Find the silver lining and make the most with what you have.

God's face appeared smiling kindly in the sky and then slowly it faded and as God or someone important retreated, etched on the clouds was the last commandment – **Love**.

Love thy environment
Love thy neighbor
Love thyself

Postlude

It all made sense to Arron now. Arron realized that not everything you hear or are told is true and not everything that you believe in or told to believe in, may be true.

He also realized having five commandments made sense. He had read somewhere that a human mind could only remember four to five things at a time. God certainly was on the ball with the commandments. Amen.

SO IT WAS ONCE WRITTEN
SO IT IS NOW BEING RETOLD

Conclusion

Hope you enjoyed reading the book as much as I enjoyed writing it. Will there be a sequel I cannot tell. If you would like to leave a thought/ feedback or want a copy of the book, please write to stories@ncipb.com.

These emails will work as well in case you are wondering. If you are a believer, use the first email. Non-believers can use the second one.

ohmygod@ncipb.com
someone.important@ncipb.com

Finally a thank you to my illustrator Stephanie Parcus for the cover. Steflynie you rock!

THE ELEVEN COMMANDMENTS?

FROM A NAKED UNSHACKLED MIND

ANNO NOMIUS

www.ingramcontent.com/pod-product-compliance
Lightning Source LLC
Chambersburg PA
CBHW031553040426
42452CB00006B/296